Annmarie Helen
xx

some²

poems by AnnMarie Eldon

some²

poems by AnnMarie Eldon

A PUBLICATION OF

BLOOMINGTON, ILLINOIS
www.mipoesias.com
October 2008
ISBN 978-1-4092-4268-0

some²

aphelion missa	11
be s	13
beyonds	14
boundaryless in bedlam	16
b()rth	17
brmm	19
concocted sangre de drago	20
corban vs. fundamental gradations	21
decision	23
deleria 2	24
deliria 5	26
deliria 6	27
dissecting the stroke	29
dry-substitute derogatories	31
eirenicons	32
epiklesis	34
floughs	35
house calls and the slattern's	36
nocturnal	38
onycholysis of the names	40
post-modern pandora's queasy turn	41
rush	42
slippages	44
statement of the hysteretic issue	46
stumped	47
tampering sacramentals	48
the banish-alternative to witches	49
the blow effect	50
the move	51
the recursive haeccity of forgiveness	54
the warrior-apices	55
there, there, but I heard different	56
to decide	58
uti possidetis	59
womb wattle and daub	63
writing the wet	65
you	66
you want the too	68
y/our affectuals	69

some²

aphelion missa

the browsweat nosed the forehead too far recompensed the unsheltering gradual the gradual externalling away the curl kernelling the repeatéds for that for that to have the wish hooked

mucous in the offingand for all that weeks thus far weeks unrevealed and the weeks further hands crazy a hand that can count bad dreams find hands wiping away a subsistuary self stroke

that comes true the wish the dream came true sorries in these words become sweat the sweat that to sweat that it takes certain uneasy no dream the icon(s) flutter their eyes a churning out more that

a sucking in potential something curdling a saliva curdling no dream opposite for that that body and and to be shirr-wished as this all chances falling away no chance to catch the blinks the Madonna patrolial no more

this body what it speaks of how it speaks that that speaking like a torture a signalling a wait for the signalling *'stretch'* a second's torture and the second splits to another a second identity which lamella-like slipes out

then from eyes to head to halo to frame to mount to wall deration all descanted by the variouses raising the toe sockets papabile rendering the knuckles reverses reciprocal no ilk for any of these yet even more

thus an immedicable madness from throat(s) but quiet so (*broke*) only whispermongers shav it these how prayers flee how keep how inilluded how already the rest-intrant scabbers ah the softs

here is here lies the introrse of my heart lover here nothing more make sheet scape claim micro-gangue from anything hollow claim me a peace kiss masseters licks lick tears tear the terrible falling sky drawing into shreds use the curtains to mop up transgressions a pirogue in the armpit danger mugenic in the falling I break I break ne'er stumble the time imponent to this calling

screed scalp bits rectiserial and thus for ever more this is how it shall be now subduction at the core all all immaterial a teredoic crawling until back and and meanwhile She eyemoves a

....oncehow spoke-how came true-how sorryso so all conflented in a blink one single one only but deskinned raw and and ice now dead-yoked it will take further a further a week

be s

before sleep katabasts a late evening deals the day's uneven palilogical errors deals deals its temporal lobes' dis-torting evidences its rheumy proclaves roomy not: tarsal creases aggravate: I

circumnavigate a preponderance to grab at straws mini-tatami pubic warmth if there would be some relieving conditions one owl might one cry but there are instead multiples

psi-falls who do transmogrify their origins with photo-fits behind eyeballs seepy jasmine might then, then The Usuals: to-be-paids history's angaric get-out-clause entendres multiples children's needs: I

try electroversioning by pre-dreaming en-couragement the last time sex was balsam poplar come, come the name of the will be new rose is red is ransomed redsum

bliss thing it was good job the lawn done snails banished iron-y smush sap-let euphoriant yet temporary brink beneath my my, my skin fornication skin-crawls: pray wash

as is its point wash away sinfuls bugmoth wingfalls pipsmash hard there is more geography for bloody tendons sackfuls hell jobs scraping intestines together unRorschaching to build indentifiables than eye-for-an-eye scores

crogcrack a fox mate trawls clamp-blink interruptions proverbial brickwalls still no empathogens between cleans nightmare tears as strassy (stars floor-floor) drieds are

plump the head's holds-all ...sink vis-à-vis the world's anhedonical 'true cause' wordwhorls: to end begin a'gain in valley flaws   *call*

beyonds

there would be belly from where pyres catbabyboys seep out
then murderous shivapsalms upending cathedraeic nipples each
one in turn showing a hand palm my god commands scuddering
along the glass surface tattecktut tattctecktut tatttetecketechetuck
corn is no use

nor willow sentimentality sunsets neither anything mountain they
dying from scrapie-likes they my shaman idoliseds who in former
times ate the choicest pick o brain pineal mushed/hippocampus
gave roasted cortex gyri to their slutslave male keepers none to

the womb-ones wombslags was their howl tied heads blind
into scarves were led unseeing into entheogen desert
peyote gatherers vomiting before enough insect
hawk made-loathsome snake snarlerers jerking off to
sand music: chief said mix 3 parts spit one part semen four parts

sand: build
token totem from whence an icarus character forlorn
wouldst make them all worms all scrawl: foresaw a voice raged
walls trains filth litter no one stands without help or sits or be s in
public and all is a deal and all is a public toilet: carve

me sitar monkeygod joker harmonica fusion I have
been down on knees when all along all else who did
penance risked death by high voltage
and pleeeze nothing with relatives
or birthday cards or wind lifting

drapes
or growing
old by the creek
or screwing behind something field fuelled
foreskin will do, something patchwork, scalp memories
how he smells of our babies unborn not fox not bear not silk not
hair not eyes especially betweens of any shape: I

shall eat dirt from beneath his toenails
and save dead skin cells in a tiny jar
embroidered in my mind's eye

'salvaged'

boundaryless in bedlam

I discover tripping over in the night my skin upon the floor. It has covered me for you for many years but a little stink of lymph drew me up. There is carpet stain I think amidst capillaries. This the token of the affair. How subcutaneous the arousal was. Your chiffoned penis head outlined against the grasp attempts its drool a pearl in pasty splatter. My sole encounters artery and extraneous andipose like the dreadful waking of erectile knowledge. Sweat glands worm their way up my legs to familiar haunts. There are green centipedes in a constant dreamline wending their way upstairs who would eat this mess. If waking from it were an option. We made an arrogance of love-making. A career. And now the basals crunching beneath a sleepwalk. I keep my blood in by uncertain denial. As if in facto esse could save me. Yet not subject to the free will of the individuals my skin has fallen off in the first attempt. My maker squeezes a corpuscle. There is a scent of sebum and lilies. The scavengers slither to a horde over boards to the rug's edge and the truth is out. This is the lore of realization. Horny and squamous I can hold together no more. I lay me down. Each pore a former glory

b()rth

this is a crivenning gutslep
how he scrivinns the dadchild myld
from me. Thence to untrapolarising: cut
scalpooze from my heart, uncorecauled. How

his was ever husband, his dread mean,
his orchestraighting
<u>all</u>ings however
did done me

fallow now only subsumed (some)days to
count scabs – donates sacri-
ficials my daughter mantra fuckyou! dad go
control else some(body) else

how
from my any God cherved, scruntised
to a babbled
         I don't say <u>grace</u>

come, girl
let's counter-parry gypsy curls
chant re-fuckyou!s and from him
take days seed reputation growth

it's okay to condemn tomorrow'll
birth comparison: I
shall receive my looks
in you Fine Child Of My Hips his

was only a piddled tadpole smaller
thanna pinhead, loathe
now, hush: blenkering a dusk prets
and genetics sivasilk, my eggs loti. No beg go: I knee-

down positioning palms which
bathed you you skin angel you so unso-so pritty
pray drusher down hope's
undeceptivity

brmm

He drove his engine into me. The fuel was humus, jasmine juice and lapis pigment. My aorta the combustion chamber. His piston upstroke was practised not in the street outside because each time I made him up in a dress and rouge with Rage Red lipstick around his nipples. He therefore had taken it apart and put it together again and again behind closed curtains but with due regard for oil and grease stains. In the confined space his exhaust spin gases were risen in the massed morning when rooks should have been. He prises something jelly-like between thumb and forefinger. Switches on. Leaves one open kiss to balm my bitten bloodying auricular helix. Burns fuel-air iron. One closed kiss to damn revolutions amongst tics who knew vibrations when they fouled the thudderless earth. And hackles trumpet bell-shaped valves. And camshaft a poison promise creeping its oval protrusions. Cam rotors careless as a strumpet's petticoats. Labia red ramsails in a rotational sunset. Talked me up crankshaft cranky. Valve springs snapped into the open position. All position. All pushrod hierarchy. And intermittent male logic which paled the toothed gear phenomena. Afterwards there would be empty rocker arms, the oscillating parts a'fire and a too obvious cylinder head. My ghostpenis on my timing belt his intake legacy. The colliding masses a droolseep upon carpet become road. The internal a sprainblue bruise. Would display mileage despondency. Would walk away. He drove his engine into me. It is still. Still here today.

concocted sangre de drago (drawing mandragon's blood)

hoodplace soothed with a thumbsmoothe move his forensics pommesmoille and coming up saffron his blank-mang slivered and candied anise in its offing shoulders proffered made-to-measure bare and sweat-larded there an autonomous cinnamon n here where his frumenty ear secret hovers you can close your eyes now I have pinned him by a bear ruse and am sallied to a froth by his helmeted coq a tart for him an unyfarced wastel waiting empty n' meaded breasts lonely as unpicked cherries crushed by a wish their verjiuce whey and salt and bittersway pasteurised by use in his complicit his thriddendele after his yes after his pointless struggle after hiparch dithers his is lord'sbread before its baking dough and all stuck yeast-lunared and mace-mad scrawning scratching all march-payne a rosquillion of rosailled fountained pearl-speds the knife still and baiting testing tethered and knocked back heady for another proving steady in our brute stealth glorious over rowles and over and simply tepid and ise-eyed and in-fere together smeggered I have him tethered in a sail-hope scounced and gaunsely all belly ready to be stuffed and prooded dreamt-drooled and alluded cornered cooked and fish-farrow knead

corban vs. fundamental gradations

taken

certain decisions are not palliative: I
squash a tiny clothes moth tentative
perhaps no more than five
mother's legacy lingers
in fluttery all sizes

moon covers a fingernail unbitten
left thumb crescented: I
label some scum of the earth
call fool watch - if watched skin curls
sum bastards

given if skin, bombblasted blood with-
drawn if fallen, fallen without hope risen
ever had: against
elderly: she calls cobwebs Irish lace
and we should need several contraptions just

to try them
dust sun gift
neighbourly: she makes
four different kinds of cake
rounds rounds egg sandwiches butter jam brown tea: on

embroidered knives shined perfect-
ly
  angled
received
sentiment: tool or cliché: I

may attempt justice
but it is out of   bounds
my hands
gaunt black orphan cries
nothing presents makeshift arms more

decent than his sharp
shirt creases smoothed to translation: I
reach grasp to understand how life portends
righteous
occlusion

my boy's brow caressed small-cool comfort (or) (for)
global shear forelengthens The Shadow's
illusion: passed
habit: passed
stubborn: passed anger: I harvest fear at least (last) unreachable

conclusion

decision

I give you your granite monument, head-high, chopped off like an unsore thumb or a giant dumb cherry. At its base it measures ten by twelve and no one is bothered. You have countered no erosion whiling away at its base. It makes perfectly astute contact with pavement, which is forever. You think you have no rut bed to lie in so you stand in a half-sleep, lolling against a knife-edge of one of its four sides, a drunken dog begging for a headache cake. Eventually you will succumb and the concrete will offer you no protection against seepage. Then stone'll suck up your warmth. In our sleep you write note form eulogies, your index finger touch burning monumentfont into impossible hardness. When you wake it's only four and no crowd. Here is your surface dependable serenity. It is off-cherry and mottled slate camouflage like a penis vein about to come alive. I give you your single life.

deleria 2

I don't know if you join a brotherhood but I think you do as repressed as a hornet's whim straitjacketed by a highwire's tensility unfair to the tenth exponent the dearth of death rare like ebola's contagion I don't think you'd dare clean shower pretend pare down to the toothplaque's stucco but I think you do unjugged hare flatfoot barebacked male jacked up and glazed over scared yet I think you do few who could look as straight as you a rainbow people person through and through I don't think think you have joined a crew yet I think you do they are lined up arranged and ready as day to consume my exhale sip my piss osmotically fit and froth and chew imbue all my kisses and shit and brew my pheromones into their own dull zombie passions if what passes for passion be drull fullbodied dredge I don't think you hedge your bets but I know you do due rent on due rent your entire life's pleasure given over to (retaliation) I don't think you bend your head in due respect no I don't think you do but plan in the deepest recesses of some hellbent retaliation some cretinous liable in slime dribble fashion keep score their suppuration a hairlip chasm in your every intention I don't think you think you let the cat out of the bag but I think you do here kitty kitty come a wall top creeping come a peeing come a poo come a howling come a sprainting come a taint arse baiting I don't think you are best placed but you do perch your little tush fair as a green eyed goblin's little hat tip bell a tinkle and a tankle and a drippy little dangle and you promised that the earth would move and you moved it too and bought a few years here and there and I don't think you took your fair share but a pox on you I don't think you are a cancer rare and incurable but I think you think you own god's decision to fashion himself in his own image demiurge the monaded surge of some hideous creation not the scourge of disingenuous I don't think you many of you are runted at the first conception but far too few and I don't think you join the countless heartbroken the clichéd fevered sleepless crying but the body snatchers and I think you do suck and not-symbiose but parasitize a scything fleecing screechering brandishing sarcasm movements as precise as laser paralysis if lasers could and yours do and metastasize your kill-fantasies into the heart of us few who have dared love you I don't think you love but you think you do I almost didn't escape but I know a thing or two about you and here I go readin' 'em out watch me though I know you do…you don't have a clue

deliria 5

what if eyes were situationally unobeyed menstruating over their cotton-clean iris yields frayed and unraveling at their into present tense dare me edges? what if like sedges swaying and replayed their slow slow make believe this is god blowing in their wind played hair   fingers more disguised and seep tears dredging out their filtered sand grit sworn pledges to stay inside besides the heart valves have not sworn to force to die but keep their up down in out temple bared deciduous engorging fall at first the first daring your limbs long bare double bound to tares paid by the tabled dared contractual exchanges forging   your dried-bayleaf-brown frenulum pushing at the eye the nail slicking back the halfmoon quick selfnailed slip bucking the   struppering false falsetto toned bewares/bemoaning grace entoning the what if and what if the braced what if the elsewhere forebeared   the nightmared compares clevered from their snigger-snares pitted to the clit-theorem budding awakening through-dares sea-mares slithering   the caissons lessening a correlating venation along arm to armpit destination a salvation a fixation murderous and special a zoning of the iridescence moulding growing a suppuration the parison possibility   glump like fire like moltening pearls like highwire chastening humbling   and all crushed hopes phenomenologically escaping into coruscation   the weeped a'sleet lubrication an asking a delectable exhortation into the what if pleading's interlunation a disappearance for difference the naturally disproportionate masturbation lineage prognostication a fatal tempering reprobatory prevarication a tuning terrible firebraked momentarily defledged childhood's dread upitting and invasive   conditions of grimace laced locked and extraordinarily ordinary once more again and the lame lain and the head bent and the spent meant memory a sedimentary stain pain and the wolves and ice and vein becomes veins a separation too too soon ordinary what if slept what if a passing a death a cursing recovery into the what ifs' deign to forgery   lewd after the asking and a crudded crust bludgeoned by a moment's rent and once more mere and once more blood

deliria 6

it goes like this not few but you many and after the spurned with who I would rather practice boundary issues yet you bend over my table with your several pounds of arse ready to be pinked up like pimentoed turkey breast the table is turmeric against your arms flesh plump as a stuffed satin cricketer's crease without its wicket I would rather practice boundary issues than fall into their embrace their little pulse race ripening to a good crescendo I go for the fat for the duck white innard for the slap for the repetitive for the reaper's aft your cleft beckons its slime smile I pace similitude along the rug's edge penury sheep coins in a field corn in a goatskin bag a prodigal reckoning the story beckons how you turned up at the door your trousers a useless disguise your shirt to be folded against torn your shoulders wearing their own roseola your rim ready I would rather practice boundary issues skim wait turn bait there is a murder scene bodies discovered grim archaeology and your sweat flekking up little shuddery micro-worms and perhaps afghanistan given a turn and a mention of some new device to catch anyone who speeds and your seeds unsettled and something male and not extra but ordinary stirs and somebody affirms some early day motions jools holland looking haggard and I won't let your fingers wander from their plinth and your offering squirms and I have birthed babies through the place where my open shut slut churns ah quoins ah scrutcheons ah chilli-burn schisms in the indecisions I would rather practice boundary issues if you'd ever put payment on this table how rich how stench nourished your feckless lack of intercourse ah pepper me pearl be girl I would unfurl whiplash clichés I would sell all tell no one I would rather practice boundary issues than confirm this could be a hatchet or a cleaver or a surgical nomenclature I would have neither weapon nor yoke your sissy swirls your bracelet distraction your fathomless need for a spokesperson on a local traffic problem a choice of channel a definite prize-winning ad all irony some tune some fad some idiotic comedian and the dressing of you goes on and on and her dad had waited for them to find her body and opera now leslie garrett with a voice slightly less cat than celine dion and I let you over your legs ajar and you manchest plumped and not bare for long for underwear on and dare enter and there is where this is where I would rather practice boundary issues buried in the brownfirm curled little hurt as ready and as coiled as a wordspring I whisper filth on queue and practice boundary issues and you and the EU summit lines up to be photographed and I enter in search of a heart and your fucksmart demeanour withers and the hurt and the carpet and the burn

dissecting the stroke

The unsurrogateable sand. The running-through fingers without ripples but knuckles. The name Clothilde not invented yet nor naming by fancies. Everyone a genealogy reputation. Suillussing demons as common as medieval leeching or almost as feed. Fish, bread, prickly pear.

But carveable sunsets into desert desist or ghee-coloured gristscapes. Each dusk an anthroposcopic pruning of possibilities. Possible the gate after a door or at any rate a corner. The corner corroded by terse strips arguing cold then heat. This world where knocking commits and other meres politables.

A shesis. A bloody turn. These burden on accounts – how many to be fed, how many drank their fill, how many days already dead, one cloak, one hem, hundreds pressing. No easy sleeping at the end. All deeds surpassable within a dark olive grove. Why don't they wait and watch?

Neither is there a wolf dawn. Prairie to the north, Alaskan cold, scritch of bear, potassium tastes and fear tang and having predatory closing-in as killers would in a clime where killers dare. Killers. They wrote in the dirt saviour killers.

Rain came and paste in the palm those words. Unproud broke the antecedeneous deer dawn. Sudden jumped atop its ill-informed false cocked dark. Which parts and thus imparts none more labile than hessian morn.

Rain came. Bend. Keep this dried. Thus on the scarious creeping, keeping corner this is how separation hides, disguised and more disguised and signisifers in soil elements, tense enough to flame at colours' scant filamentation. But skin. Rain came and rubbed.

Eonsed-over and saints to be made. But rubbing rain came. Bought the prickly pear up. Ran anyway. The baptismal pre-flood calm so small in the rubbed. Same water which rubybrown sinstain swayshes.

Only once and all the curdle torrent seeped. Barely perceptible. Love in a current. Innard-screams scravle the peace. But not before diamond micro-whorl and fingerprints of bloods stroped a tiny tear hope.

dry-substitute derogatories

So it is a dayscape. You must decide. If you are to decide for dry you must identify yourself. Which side. For placenta or grouse-supper rituals. Otherwise slow soporifices. Marigold. Caraway. Poppyhead. Their succour strength undiminished by ground, by hard. There is a caul in the offing. Vacillating do the blubber vanes gather. They are known by humps. By what they contain and their pressure evidence. That the gather-reflex has predominated. They are steer differentiated. You must get up a war party store against the line decay. A smudge for every time the fingers have touched. In the shallow muds clarity is not a choice but a privilege. A silver spoon in the river mouth. Watch as it eases a passage out. You must intend also on direction. To sever your entire service-sense you call up the foam animals. They gather in storm circles. The clouds make séance. Then from the crisps they have come. From the scather banks. From easterlies which made even the tongue stick. The roof of the mouth was its best bet. Could not even whisper for alleviation. And swallow a pipe dream. But still the swim-legs come and all manner of relatéds. Counting them a chore unresisted. But resist you must. There is a line. The black line. The black line cuts through everything, everything delayed, especially spiral capable things, those which blossom, those which degenerate, those which point blame, those which honest with no context. It requires a taste steady for gore-gazes, those killer eyes seeking to core. However, it is you who has forgotten more sunsets than there was sky for. Though gut-sad it doesn't stop. Is strong in consistent. Here again the dermis-dependents. Watch for the hawk-carrier signs. The iceglint in the eye. This comes from compressed things which are neither side of the line. All nondamp. All reconsigned in a terrible hurry so that the final word can be gotten in. And this not like a living-harvest which needs chopping. Nor a gathering. Nothing No mucousy cover. No fungi outgrowths. No humus extra. So then to dry after all. It should be in blood but is in a slight tilt of the head. All wakes to the dread-levelling hint. And all shrivels before the consequentials. Despite light your look through the maul-slips. Not one bit that isn't written on the wall. Your call.

eirenicons

particle/wave
hedera a dank viridian helixed: or
snowberry which perhaps may hide, feed pheasant in any
case bamboozle the dormer: which wind
north north easterly: or
westerly a utilitarian oddity: or
its own suckering chirality: or
I hunt my click-clackless sheets for you my silent
screwed

lustre
no, nothing but lack-
fashionable black and whitish
with its blurb about a Pavlov's dog
a Schrödinger's cat some novel: I don't
to read your: dead caecilian lose momentum down
my thigh: I'm a lopsided
callipygian because of it: I
don't buy the stupid book
neither could: I make a recommendation but you come damn
good

lumen-aether
onto: banks ditch-spoil has been cast: up
these now chamfered for nesting/song posts
anything wider than: wrist coppiced
hawthorn, hazel, dogwood whips n bare-roo
ted saplings in quills: 3 or 4   miles: or
giant's stubble giant's stubble giant's stubble: or
diloginous pricks: you never
forget to shave each:
morning

Descartes' ray
simple errand this: journey from whence slopped

iridescenses
hay when summer burns God knows a mutugen midden un-
dredged spurge is the rainbow's end position or momentum?
also seemed not to: know where you hell were
where you hell were blackcrow or: gold downs hypolimnioned
hell crap pot when: it
hurt

supernumerary arcs
somebody left up their Christmas tree lights: outside: ones
rain-on-them rained on
they appear crystal turians pip pips spider bum
spunned but now do not: turn them on
present present you present yourself
for the taking: of

meleagrinae
to… it should be a simple task
to gloss over threatening snow
to forget the mow and weave which may: appear: so
but with much sweat in grass which we bet there are: many
stomachs for but don't know how
the count goes cud plough mow
or the wardrobe order
or bookcases you: seem fit
eat this forget bile collodions, forget
smile

photon-s
to this house was not written *canonically*
conjugated quantum
you will return
as if 5 yrs
read

'rule of thumb'

epiklesis

waking's pecuniary insistence
necessary medication ground coffee my: mouth around it
not debunking Freudian inheritances
but dawn allotted perseverance

M40 motorway quadratic equational railways
too many: counties to draw lines by
kiss become separation become Choc-o-late Chip Cookie
become:
crumb

eventually the Schumann Fantasy in C
medieval isosceles scattered
in diocesan regularity: a
spidery sun minding how we go: so

despite impossible domestic scalenes no: fatalities
this time: exchanges, dichotomous
from within and between which we shall (some)how
become our own

sort of: triune unity
sort of:
sum

floughs

why slated? it pitch it jet it unseeable tilt enterable zest a constant Cézanneing ochre burn and satin-pith cream broth female sperm scent unimaginable except as unquench so that his knees bleed his hands Vermeering for dull grub-bing interior browns a release dull stinking musk myrrh wrap himself in any friggingFrink-intaglio any ChaucerTales print white moonscapable cool blue but my guttural hole throat swells crystally slide there he wants touch epiglottis spot punch angles meld held by scalp blackmail anything tile-like or homely for a split no kind of any kind second all he saw was moon against guttering a reeve hem a gloved oesophagus welcome hot smelt my smile wiped him from my corner licked slipped mouth pipes copper cold but their history was forever velvet mouth fucked framed it improbable it click broke wept gathered skitty-hem what was natural two him - *soon* he'd said (fuck-reference: no oxalissy toottoot open close pointypeck pecks this time/year all dead seeming underground yet) *tts would* run fingers t'entice *ooh* galanthus spermy tip nivalis clump nerves along my spine drip drippy narcissussy combine droop head with always my sublime thirst after my come my spurgy tears our hi-tech back-nowness but hell, would fescue <u>me</u> first

house calls and the slattern's self-disparaging emesis

a soul accouchement skin febriculae torque pre-intuitively: at first sight a trismus always slight tremouring: as night stars seen through dusk's unforeseen femerall permitting: a brief bad bad capnomancy then the vagus nerve gone: and

breathing never the same again but for years: a love that shook cephalic reasoning tore genetics foreswore silence kept vision visual until visceral and could no more who could ever know the river of the long tides: a

crow grating hisnhoarseradish call across the shore: its protected piping plover blowing back a shrill schoolyard whistle: in sweet disregard miles by thousands unbargained for: and all forfeited there was to be a conversion a supination long before: the

costive tears bludgeoning forth beneath the fourth station twisting lives together gathering signs such as wondered upon: a wooden cross engraved with a family name still there dried: to greyed ivory a settlers' graveyard brim full of marble granite: and

pocked red sandstone with most graves babies' some dead before they lived still others dying in the order they were born dates barely readable ghost years the cholera's claim: a universe trephined away from domestic certainty: a

nyctalopia on both parts for parental responsibility semen spilt aeons across multicoloured dawns I think of myself as 'him': a necrosis of what kept me hardened now brittle how much I have loved him there is no possible asnosmia within his lecturing mode his turning

me seduction a desquamation of resolve are only slovenly hills: are slow easy-wide lanes a half-hour but nothing against the megrim's advance relieved by my whoring my mouth off each day checked off produces: a slight palpebral apathy feigned days days relieved by the menarche when I already witched him and faith here always the familiar paresis: a surdity for children's needs: a foetal curve which erases no need ungual tracks upon the softest unreceivables ours: the

same shadow sharing the same asthenia dangerous miles: to have come to numb a forced xerosis an imperceptible lysis enough to fake normal I pine I beal: the present no sensational novelties simply routine no one died of a broken:

heart but always from premeditated error: or error: or fatal intrusion bacterial some immunological rationality how absurd the allocheira shared or imaginary some other woman makes laugh now in time I shall say I am: wounded walls plastered: a presentable pus slackens their: verticals

these same walls from whereout there is no hope: of travel: or release retchback I love you how I love you

nocturnal

The cold-forged nails are our waiting. We make panels around our isolation. Of it the spikes are already driven into pailings upon which the rain coats and runnels against the separating boards. The boards are sodden and turning to tissue. The stomach understands this and we inhale the liquid as sweat. Sweat is simply itself contained within itself within the rain so there is only squeam-surface and that as cold as cold and more rain sheeting too and against that the only barrier a glazing and thus to glazing sprigs ice sharp as the night falls and sprittled through the stomach hope. We have to batten down somehow even though no equipment for it. They dole out everything we need the sleep carers and thus make the nailing down more far off as morning could be. But we have the ice fields to traverse and later mountains so as for the heaven feel we are practical with all things woolen and multiple layers and even the catch garments have tiny tacks somewhere within their seams. Pins too. Whence the water falls the clout nails appear along the edges of the fixing slates. We are compartmentalized for the handing out and the galvanized dreads come and something akin to anti-nausea the slight beckoning slope of it so enticing from the ground the dirt wire mesh to get through to get to the field the field of our making the ruts of it. Our rolling the black rectangular details. The reached-switch machine would make a film of the nailing but it is as loud as drums the endless cut and endless in number the endless tacks the water down. Sheared from our joint slaking the stakes backed up against our ankles and only a singular tension and no disassociation not grouped for any map start and no one to pull back and no one to remind and no one. All the moisture a gut capable droll hammering of it of foaming at the mouth's expense of the temples of pulse points in the elbows' crooks whenever we are grateful. The hands out for pliers to recycle the nails by but only a dull steel-like smudge where the moon might be. The rose-head nail a swallowing the wrought nails the throat snails slow the choking then the roof of the mouth a overhead hazard which threatens to slip in its dry like a terrible tearing or a tear-duct tare the zinc-scream of it waking alone in a sigh of loose tiles slithering to at best a claw tool vein threatening the terror. It cannot happen so the moon is sluiced away. To where here broken between the dissolving panels where taken to fixing between saturated withies the walls half-holding despite pleadings the bleeding shins marking descent there again there each step. And a hand's breadth gloved yet loveless trek. How slow memory hoardings melt how low-abandoned for loving for wanting it to hold together. Cannot nail must glue pelts how spent how bowed the hell-bent head the alloy allowance waned. Squarer now and with a single throw all offers useless and a no no no.

onycholysis of the names

there *might*'ave been some way to distinguish my: lunula
smile from the whites of my eyes: I a mother a keratinned
heart who has sloughed off my husband's dried curdle past
the old stone butler

sink's skin clockantiwise into an impartial open disinfected: drain
my vascular cambium disregard phloemming, renewing that:
'public' self: thunder nights, when granny hides house knives
under-
stair, *she*, (her mother's daughter) force feeds me: her

children grandad's rum with hot water 'n sugar xylems her: there
there dear dear little sapwood spoonies-fed whilst the: wind
beneath door crackedseals ghaspps *eponychium eponychium
eponychium*
my: sister my other self distalled addicted a labelledlong a me list
smooth,

furrowed, plated, warty, fibrous, papery, barking oh for crying out
it should be possible to trace the family tree without pointing a
finger

post-modern pandora's queasy turn

I: cosset first the tangled bed wire
then leftover hair tourmaline yet mattressed
and on through decadent dried scars, severe,
sculpted, forming waves with each a nauseate
as if: sincere at the time: thus not solitary
but compacted: hence far too much to simply
surf and so: stacks discarded sincerities
brutal attempts at recompense all those many:
many times I'd tried but you said in:
defence suddenly huge like a David brilliantly sculpted
out of a thin thin block exact rebutted
strange that: how clever he is
artistic 'ologies in their own Tunbridge ware marquetry
protection
precisely inlaid history dark exceptions against our: lighter
shamless selves many moves towards a middle ground
lush skin scents counting as smaller, finer *objets* com-
pacted bejewelled alongside a wry smile
an ironic agreement as-seen-from-inside
matching fabrics domestically designed timetables
forthcoming and driving together to pre-arranged relaxed
destinations as if another purpose as if again enjoyable
as if with written stuff jazz that was understood classical that
wasn't grotesque shouted Germanic whining Italianate
melodramatics anything Wagnerian and inhalations adhered to as
yet: another gorgeously wrapped also the biggest *ehm* as if: as if as
if: a prayer as if: a tropism and I: could dare and fuck it and
chuck it all

rush

this is the fall of it the eyes didn't follow the phook grendadinary of it the complicit fallows the distempered reconnoitres what are the ousted stays the ones the hands didn't the way they stayed in pockets the terrible inhibit also others'

these ways are the ways of the heated tempers they should go over unraveling past stations and not of the cross not any number fourteen fifteen or invented more these are train stops and not metaphor track ends

these are the link muscles pierced these are the heart tremors muspering their susupenses these hearse-ways the stare blocks the shoulders not quite curse-brushing the stranger-days there too could be ice in the clink-pools no One to care so

packice forms in the nether cracks and sesquemious strands and the unmartyred the pyre stain the widow shadow the other way the branches felled with no axe upon no steady rays the fingers durst not play

dust in the alley trays and all else thrown out rooks scavenge as loners this against nature and even wrists remain up to the elbow in leaf temper and a cold mould upon their crease risk hills make governance dreams

dreams where palms as full as pomegranates a sublimation gathered beneath a store of random misses the unplanned by cloudful straightway to the spine she squats as a mountain gnat to sustain the time to wait to uncurse spit settled

his voice but part only like whisper rains a possible of cold but furlongs yet the forethought spare change clinks in the rowted care places grips grips fervent if need a face now as a sign now as a population now a named grid reference not mere number but Solomon's song source the pendulum's triangulation see how the windows meet the shunt redeplorable for spines to coalesce all tremooring all clamooring for moist cheek-lace the course the deep-well the suckplace the more-strange the met-curse the

long long road the sway the undulating bed creases slumber lack projected scree slopes slight hitches skin flakes sweat for the asking mace-mordant fogs rift valleys full of pride sloughed pedigree smiles all fake hindrances stepped aside sullies and the rucked sheets and

tears joined too precipitation enough to oasis the prayers' populace gifted a trinity sowersing this this-river sense there where there is something pubic in the private ravine dogs scent for it heaven obeys with a folding star seen latterly to careen wolf and bane together

far overdue display of destination in the pupils' reflections each iris having a vanishing point formerly supplication becomes the only harbor he he goes down and. Far and. Again overdue on knees and makes a curse enquiry the ley lines preamble doors open to let

the crush screams hover there is excess just as the clouds give out her juice is the bone carcass meadow grass and we, we go marring to the final tamarind'd lush-smell to foul upon the path we spraint as the doves would if they were ghouls all eyes

feign tempt to torture risk take the hands from pockets find the pulse-pace between blade hills fill the space between leg valleys follow the trail between need ravines the haste forswears it much crave-taste it broils and binds the co-fellows tumble it the Only only follow-chrism it

it trust dares it it swallows this touch placated hope bares it nothing to hallow except the constant the constant sunken tremble the now-parting calumnies the far-ardent creamy white samite jizz of her asking it their arms wild-linked the forlorn undefiled more taxing of the unborn child

slippages

take the lover's words at their most adroit
for this is the lathering welcome soft
as liquorice froth on a bed of fished
rice where no manplan followed
the dead harridan's line

for this also where the massive daddy longlegs
memory crawls contemporaneously
with one mind you only massive rose thorn
made dreg-veined legs
could not yet crawled

curled up nurserybed-wise and sleep tested
against the cutting point her birther's hands
and shouting mouth how they were hacking
the hedge down and failed to notice no sand
notice no

come sea time there are whoosh angels
in scampering tides clithering backwards along
the shoreline so gets us to find ourselves and words
they have slanted somewhat from the cruel pagewise the

trail stockings dirt as journey in nylonny
as dredge shimmying pathfinders led his coming
tomorrow the where this fits on over the carbonated granite
clevvages the oily rain washes sense into
to ravage the thought ravage to

find ourselves holds like a huge holding pattern over
their circling the planes the hedgepicky blackbird scrawbling
his very very very nice to see you how the worm earth provides

to have the cleaning taken from her not her sister
who sat at feet who smoothes tears who taught
with precious perfume offering
whose five languid are
carefully unhook

from the scripts now life is in
the sand
the leaf
the fingercrusting because

they ache for a skin surface not the antiskin
teachings after all not anything fallen but glossy
as if kedgeree became constituents again
and mad mother actually died no scratch-trench

most: to rest is to believe it can be given
to believe is to was not reborn in the genes
is to found not self but demiocean simply was
washed was peacesalt held was real-laid not churned

statement of the hysteretic issue

and yours is the afterthoughts' begging the where the schist boulderhaven is not the shoulder slime place but the nonsupport of it so hurt so only down and hers would be the old of it and his the roughworn nylonny equivalent of sack and of that of how swelled-over by the disaffects are not illiterate poor but middles with self-cause and if a we could fathom the hem to unstitch could make the swelling pushing crowd subside to audience but wouldn't want that because they they the ones who happened to be there and we we the ones who for a tacking runningback by machine now in invisible thread the morning dread swell to ask by what power nightmares wakened over their breadtime and yours is the whennevers' dregging the fraggonarded Cicero world the dam unbreaking but studied care-fully and-fully intended so there must be a hers even if crippled it is obverse this seduction: your style don't matter who-hurt it go "bag those untittied crusts/don't never think of share/share one of them feelwords" how unprepared how naive how this lavaslide a fuckinghell curve a swerve against all justification how reelrell-nettéd we all the sweat pits save-me, save-me to the nose the rose no saviourspit as it withers deadlining to the old old old of it of it the bendslump slithers to an afternoon repeat borders refugees tornlimb-tatters wretcheds weep no wreaths one kiss would do it and the strength would drain dwells, dwells in the hands' and we the ones we the choice blatherers we the bared eye for eyers not cheek but why answerers we the fedcentre certainters unending pretend retaliators look love how rimmed-over by the thudsudden recognition cardiac sensory neurites how lost in the slopblood pools pools of our tears makes like a cult arrhythmias (*oh shit* all oneGodbelievers afterall...) danceswirl my man-gal firmaments dearth damn you sneggering I skip a fall beat and ours and ours is the underworld-afterthoughts'

stumped

no few trees my forest tresses have lain
foundation, ill-neatly compass their trail
unbridle pathways reign deep enbriared
versions of more formal

sheltered selves. Root snaps where
'praps it should heed canopial obligations
boundaries branch and desist, turn
head, scabber weathered
hands furrowing for prayer

rules left fallow go hybrid to seed
I scatter rust to feed children
thus I'm marked wisdom, chained cook-pot
I cloth up spots of the world's water-
falling irreg
ularities, hack freedoms

from some indebted dead
wood. Focus upon each just-next silkstain
there may be nightshades of uncaring
I shake barbs. Take leave

(of) myself. Place weight on
empty spaces. Strain along borrowed boughs
stake one step along ancient trusts. I know
not how unhefted needs grow
earth cries a fossil tomorrow

plains beckon

tampering sacramentals

wearing horsehair down shirts
to dog spin-thrift: I
ply splinters make smooth floorboard expanse walk
night plank thus uneasy
logicality: Maritain, Jacques, his imprimatured
proprieties unfamiliar steps. Late
then and tired
    and then fuck the theology bed
    and drift
    and baccatéd pasts lump dreams a:
dread sump next: day
bunion aches callous corn dare off
cold scrape some thing stick-
y under: foot straighten not altar but: table
cloth lest veer sieve thanks stay: put as: morning: breaks
staples bread test a-
head

the banish-alternative to witches

The witches are our ship. Its deck the sea. We lie upon a thin sheet, undulating with the waves, our knees bent into backs of knees where no anatomy names. Sail north against an east coast. Dare wind to drive the counterpane, tugged around chins, ears. We are warm in shared exhale only; the saltdamp searching, seeking between warp and weft, the crest and fall increasing. Seafetch ransacks all intimacies, skin in shiver spots; we tweak blankets to pretend the cold out. Whitecaps whisper in circles above their horizontaless conspiracy and in dreams even the surfzone freezes. Invent a net, contrapted to hitch up against prevailing ice. Ice forms upon its mosquito-surface. We must risk an arm above the bed to tackle a lone, dank haulribbon. Ease it over our numbheads. Uncanter indown within it. Block ice now, outbalancing the wire sprung rim, biting into mini-hinges. Snap it to susurround us. Hang on every indulge to fasten. Yet it bends with the weight of ice. Make the mordant bedding a slivering pine to balance on so that the psyche may recover. We are naked yet the surface solid. Use the soles to tread down any wave formations beneath us. The wiremesh bed husk turns a pale sycamore-cream, becomes bee-keeper gauze, the entire ship ensunned by protection. Ice on the outside lends heatsuck to bare goosedflesh. Pretend heat and the ship can sail on north, slicing ice flows, all mock-hull, flimsy wood and crushable. Turn. Turn the ship to metal. Turn the ship west across the arctic line through obstacles more terrible than diminutive iceneedles into every pore. Sailing steel needs soft. Pull hoods. Pull skirts. Pull sleeves. Pull wraps. All clothing nondescript flimsied atop the head, heads in a chorus. Knuckles masks. Peer out between vista makers. Ponder upon. Drop anchor. At random, dock. The witches little shrivelleds. Make drust. Make seed. Pay heed to blow the deck clean. It is drying in patches where the breath spots. Try stay as a concept. No hay as yet. Nor rock. But home anyway. Take stock.

the blow effect

I shall hide my fear in the reactor chamber. This is not the same bedroom we use for fucking in but a self-sustaining, steady place refurbished with purple-carpeted walls to flux the death chains. My loneliness is neutron heavy and suggested on paranoia alternatives yet he can second-guess the heavy/light water alternatives with a sniff of the gusset a mile away. It's true there's no coolant in the veins and only output but he was dressed in satin and saliva-stained nylon and tested and tested and then disappeared so what am I to think? I have my run shift ready at all times even when there are tears and especially when these classified according to appropriateness. It used to be daily, the fissile nonsense. There were random statistical variations based on whether there was a leftover smell of rubber and periodic variations by the moon. Of course the operating parameters have reverted to his side now. I understand analogue depression. The effects of adult attachment disorder upon the core. The parameters mean shutdown. Zero trip amongst the sodden tissue memory. The screw room can be as hygienic as surgery would require. Control rods all in place and a living breathing antiseptic zith from one old movie or more. Cloth. Rags. The ancient art of scrotum cleansing, graphite moderators, the rewriting of history. Mixed metaphor. I assemble the dildo, thong, whip, gag and stretch cord until a change of reactivity is caused. Their removal means the funereal walls reverb no more. Unity is measured in different ways. Tuesdays or handkerchiefed jizz. Recently a high grade steel and tungsten mix and a pectoral shift. No irradiadic remorse. Old fashioned morbidity. Penciled resolutions. I shall lie down in the room next door.

the move

he took off his belt so that the buckle wouldn't scratch
and removed other sharp objects from his person

he did not find out how the furniture had been
put together. Nor did he look for any parts that could be

detached. He didn't study the route to use or locate
anything that would cause trouble. For example light fixtures
jutting out the wall

he may have lifted the furniture where it was strongest
however the glass table-
top he moved without the route being cleared of obstructions

he didn't wrap it in a blanket to prevent any damage items
needed on a daily basis were simply pushed to one side without
regard to
their being delicate or

fragile. He didn't help me decide exactly where he would place
anything
the temperature of the new locations was much higher and a

sudden and extreme variation in humidity
threatened

nothing was moved slowly or carefully. The
armchair bumped against the doorway, the walls were marked

he didn't hold the sofa firmly. It almost slipped from his
hands. He slid and then dragged it along into

the alcove and perhaps the boards were scratched and certainly
the carpet
torn

obviously no careful or meticulous planning so neither of us examined the
sideboard for loose joinery and didn't remove its
                                                                shelves or

drawers. A highly polished occasional table was lifted, not by its
legs, but by its top, which threatened to come
off
the dining chairs were lifted by their arms

as for essentials - kettle, tea bags and coffee, cups, bathroom supplies,
towels, mobile phone recharger, first-aid kit, these

were scattered by a fierce and intrusive wind, which had no regard for
emergency
yet everything also *slow* and meticulous

the bed got dragged across the yard, as excessive lateral pressure on its legs
caused them to
shear

and although the fridge and freezer emptied and defrosted themselves, because the bed was out of action, there was no correlation to
anything and we had to fuck

on the floor. All the windows   flew open
the appliances became unplugged. The neighbours forgot which day

it was
only the books
lay flat with alternate bindings preventing spinal
        damage

otherwise there were bruises and blood
clothing had no consciousness for hangers bodies closets or drawers
arms and legs as one

temporarily all the electronics switched on
histrionics. Hysterics. It was not a case of separate, or bubble wrapped or
inkless or safe in anyway whatsoever. Pads, bowls, hollows, suggestive

materials. Screams. Scratches. Lots and lots and lots
                  of scratches

then layers. Layers and layers. Tears. Tissues. History. Small and large without regard to time or carcass or suitability

God in the newsprint. Chaos down
wires
upright position where possible. And not possible. Until

afterwards
labelled: reclosable

smears gone and the hair in place
blankets on and a few scuffed smiles

the recursive haeccity of forgiveness

there are: subterfuges, latent across: carpet. Singular
hair, once heads skin by its nature entopic now
hidden as weft as: I pan through panes to: ground thistles'
flowering remains and remember: wet and: vest and: put on specs
and: go out to inspect and: find intrepid cinquefoil creeping
alongside my best efforts
try to disembroider past from now: postpartum apples pears
wasp: bitten
my own hair a nest. At best back
to inside. To front some sort of: death
in the terrible tryingness
leftovers akairic I: suppose as the 19.08
kettles on a balmy slight south-south-west: detergent suds pets
begets him his conspicuous ambition/logically circular defences
bagged and hung like pheasant waiting stink. Passed: trepid spots
where grease met children's finger tips
soggy, indiscreet substances
goose grass stickies
tired: a fog, a betrayal dog-eared promises: yet
heady 'memberences
eyes: heft
smitten.
softing planes, blames: rewritten
and sex, always sex
blessed really with arms at: the ready
even on the brink
and at: last, steady
and: steady
and steady

the warrior-apices

you got down upon your knees and began to count your
strategies ababa a-grain-of-sand
ahaha dust-specks-in-a-sunbeam
nirabbuda rabbit's-grain
abbuda ram's-grain
vibhutangama ox's-grain
sarvajna poppy-seed
bindu mustard-seed
sarvabala barleycorn
mudrabala rabbit-egg
niravadya sheep-egg
akkhobini ox-egg
gananagati eggs-in-a-basket
samaptalambha eggs-upon-a-roof
hetvindriya eggs-within-a-cloud
ninnahuta clouds-within-a-sky
hetuhila skies-upon-a-turtle-back
vyavasthanapajnapati black-wishes-squashed-by-white
titlambha white-wishes-upon-a-grain-of-sand
nahuta sand-upon-gratuitous-compassion
nagabala compassion-upon-loneliness
bahula tears-cried-in-loneliness
kotippakoti holiness-upon-tears
vivaha a palmful-of-holiness
kshobhya prayer-unspoken
vivara prayer-upon-a grain-of wickedness
pakoti wickedness-upon-a-grain-of-sand
kankara homeland
niyuta heaven-in-a-sunbeam
ayuta the-all-inclusiveness-of-and
koti and placed through torn cloth a finger-and-thumbful of
spittle upon each grazed knee and stood and went about
your daily business

there, there, **but I heard different**

bidden inside depths spear reasons
depridated before they've a chance
by agreement we know faces made
famous by how they present. Where

now my intent that I try: razoring
pulling on mind-string terribly
invisible: attached to my mouth
gibberings my moustachioed tries: if

I had such such-things. Aagh Christ tug
lug little metal clippy clips through November's
slimings. Pollarded planes, trunks camo-
uflaged, bark that needs flogging

river flood reeds dominatrixmising
back to edge. I know there's money
to be made if one looks correct, fame
tussling clobbered pale milkmaid types. A List:

hypes
high flyers
rushy feminine nomads looking for a shop window
to live right in. How much shall we abide by? Tyres

squish. If I: slow it all down and keep keep keep
hoping I can achieve it my task my it today it task get this
iron clinker out this tree stump keep alive this love this bad
stomach bug crapping down me he looks familiar he looks: he

presents he doesn't ask What holds the sky up? doesn't *ghh*asp
doesn't rasp an 'in' as a rare red hawk glides on carrion
hustle/thermal
is black and grey and whitey shades and clout and normal
and once was *oh so*

but truth is: sap. Now there's a thing
it's not vital it's: fallen
leaves foot slopped. To where dog hair does or ('Again:')
children's sticky finger marks loose change buttons
spare sun to be glared by incandescence of: any kind
prayer sung silent whispered angry twins separated from birth
today's bread on the table hymn tremors "Mommy I love…"
angel appearances milk glop curdles

down drains I suspect
yet watch how we deflect
a murderer invents a bath-time story
still, haloes like halogen promises: there must be a heaven I:
know this because I could *there* one-finger-one-thumb this safety
pin from my magic tree
and find all the tut-tuts, misgivings, those times I failed to forgive

found my Losts my naiveté
a man ugly uninteresting steady not-Spiv-slick-oily
my real meaning
not just encompass them
but burn 'til: molten
entitled "Magdalene's Nitrobenzeney Ultramarine Compassion"

to decide

the fastidious foldingness of all things softly becoming one a fleet of angels wings flashing moonbeams seawaves made from silk froth desisted and flattening down upon itself eiderdown cheek hair crushed by leeward breeze moans a monad upon its carressful carefulling sop masses by the wenchhair curls

unceremonious contact as if forever gone by on a tear one eyeful crescent pearl a blink a chink in the stare armour careful too to blush so synchronistically both reddening the shoulders shelves for sobpools and excess crawls in slowmotion stop-drool then the acre-aches the terses

a curse atop a sigh a sigh for each phoneme how resisted temptations eventually cave in how decided that how predestined and limed too by a white hot caulking of the heart's excesses so petals wither whence before them a scent of the holy sent freely

firm also as if solid this ruaching and a druidtone set across the tidetops each sargassoing no more just so so for the moon-pulls and no timetables to rely upon and all earth aroar with one implacable undeciding girl type turn

seeps the silence the intrusion voices the blood stain soaped down to a dull earth all rendering to cliché the inert foragers for a cheek check the cheap repeat blush sturls reddening some other places so to oiljiz furls how spurts

how fluids can govern a spasm when the body-crevices so much smaller than planet whorls turn, turn, turn look upon and again upon this and a terrible gainless mess and say if we made disaster or lives or a flood or shone light into unanswerable pretence

uti possidetis

I am dreaming his psyche for him a bed in the shack's end rickety fences walls beyond these males go about business sorting mail and handing out orders to sleep against their voices one street coming down to the north to sleep beside a drugged figure in another bed who succumbs to the same dreams passing work to sleep it off work to wake work to walk the two beds' short widths to the outside world to the west work to work at the counter to work the queues who want to post who hold cards scraps of paper letters and more formal and less formal devoid of envelopes invitations but all need stamps the daily job to wake the sleepless dreaming and walk beyond the shack to stand behind the counter and serve stamps when all is wood planks boards planes and broken and creaking and gaps and swaying in the increasing wind because the sea comes from the north and the west and it must be a special conjunction according to gossip the people who stand in line and wait with paper in hand who wait to send have theories about the sea why the sea encroaches upon the shack yet indulge in speculation too to stand on the wrong side of the counter money in hand to buy stamps but where any letters are not known and trading confusion the boss busies himself with his subordinate's role but does not know who should be there does not recognize the worker by night the dreamer by day and the dreamer is knifing away old candle wax to go away money in hand and lie down again upon a shack bed lone dreamer and the sea is in from miles away it washes up blubber animals from its deep and there is no foam only the firm waves edging and a faint sea mist creeping in the shack's dilapidated boards some slight droplet upon the pillow's edge and a salt damp seeping into covers like a truth dawning these are not dead the heavy rolling little sea animals getting larger as the sea gets closer as the wind opens up the gaps as the board walls creak and bend and the far off men's voices become more factory and there is the decomposed ready to swell narcoleptic squalor the task chosen for he could not ask but both supposed from one arm's length passing as shoulders turned back to the engulfing sea the sea passing its safety zone no he dared not slip the mask but is all those the one who foetal permanently dozes the unseeing scurrying boss who knows the brief all those who write and wait and whose waiting goes nowhere except back again and again to the real work and could not slip the mask but skin not a strategic joint initiative but in this a private venture the wicks are those parts with no resistance with nailess wood and caskless soul sent the heaviest task the only protection one whole rough greywool blanket against a shoal of stinking truths where his weakness gets in this no duty handed down upon a battered platter by the maker's hand but one which was forgotten objects chosen animately presenting themselves as sacrifices to this task and being everywhere it appears more than a forgone conclusion but a sole purpose it smoothes domesticity into clean lists it is extreme in caution in the sharp areas in chores in the not yet tangible the sheets the creases no no joint crying for a shared domain none permissible hands cojoined yet unsaid shares his way never to head through its own too fast-smart passing places also run-on thoughts pillows whatever he can't speak about laid there the unslipped intermittently a surprising tearing the sea intimacy lymph the gaps sweated a due-to gradient to rise with a cloth in hand but whether to clean or scour the mask and what and all the eyes cast down and his arms remoting trust his ether escape my mary prayer and I am patient dreaming his psyche for him

weight of the running white

breasts milkful children grown and almost gone somewhere no
doubt horses with their rumps to horse-doors which they don't
know there's a word for bolted as if something from the blue

although breast milk is whiter than white like Cézanne's scratches
in the too bright light not the filmy white or pearly white nothing
mixy about breast milk as if it's on the boil always and bursting to
come up in the pan whiter than white until it foams and escapes
the huge pressure of the nipples

nerves too as if sucking is something horrendously universal as
if all the world depended on its pressure this pain and still the
horses stand with their rumps to doors all the wrong language as
if also can be replicated over and over and over as if as if not a
dream as if

not in a dream state but a good honest misplacement of choice
why horse? why plural? as if one were not enough as a picture as
if other pictures could fill in the blanks all the times waiting all
the times alone all the empty arms and why many many arms as
if two were not empty enough? and why rhetorical

when the answer is at hand arms hands a word at the fingertips
all body parts co-joined by the limb the generic limb arm as
if reaching and swimming and holding and dying were all the
same yet arms don't rush legs do

and legs legs are pearly legs may be painted in shades of white a
translucent or a zinc and never white but peach and grey and
bruise and green and purple and the entire palette because legs ah
legs

legs like Michelangelo's Adam skewed at a terrible angle simply to
show off the torso a male torso twisted as if to give birth and
pregnant with muscle and here the one horse turns too and
shows a side rump which in horse terms has a word has has

the artist as moment-manager never late always on time painting emptiness the moment the entire empties not just the two arms waiting for fill and now two artists and more than one horse and too much filler and yet not enough

and it is possible to ejaculate and not orgasm you say and the world spins on a cue you early but not knowing of it and a gap opens and there time slips its hand into the event of your coming

and slows enough so that the horses lay down and graze in sudden fields mountain singular God winks as well as points and there's an ache less dull in the breasts than it was perhaps enough for the starving to creep into or seep, seep

womb wattle and daub

in order that s/he cling too I send out posts upright
between these oughts: oak staves
my fill subsoil, straw on good days
or cow-dung and lime. Whatever...

s/he'd weave withes, willow thoughts
that s/he'd slither wet meandering
through my tough home hessian-here
used to hold til dry. A wall

on which would be nought
but tedious historicity, perhaps a house front facsimile
not sturdy though like lath and plaster
but crack-faults for soft lap laughter moon lather. 1

night some slight unplanned imprint
of dedicated buttercup fossilled star
so hollow it fleshed a beholdened path
mirroring t/his sigh

well tired so very tired and all along alone
s/he faltered but high so unstrong s/he'd cry,
use tears' salts to keep a steer by. I tipped tongue
and rimmed a cum-corona around t/his stockaded clearing
tumbling

to trust because ancient because weak because distant because
half-asleep because stranded revealed dead kings crazed tombs
where solitude had brazened them. Trenches
which bore children. Fears rodomontaded. Some-*thing*

gold. At which s/he tore
s/he it was who riddled plains for fools, forswore
the use of knife. It is a dermisal device. I cannot find it in any
book my love. Help me. Who clawed t/his shroud to heaven
threads spun out t/his

sodden horizon sinking fell from
dread to gather handfuls of stippled diamond drool stinking, bled
birth emblem emblazoning lecouroheal trail led and asked, "Why
are these trees like webs in the lamp's light dear?"

and t/his question s/he followed back to roots to slatted-keep
as strangers do who have only modern
moment-moated clues to cling to

writing the wet

obfuscating rain: not quite grammatical
to ground nor from source indetermined
then severely again as if heaven sentence
each grain saccate falls to heave a'second
or thrice-upped squiff nor marks separate
but all conjoined the dry forevered out: I
the in vain attempt hair scrouted down to
merely a hands crunched necessary uneasy
protuberance-set: let skin shift compenses
by dint analysis suckers pukcour their out-
throat needs: too much drink, too milked,
too satiated too: short shrift do clodclouds
something more: sour damp frails its own
drill, drill-squeemster promisary: walls run
slivers and dalmatic at that pore-pout: mist
a clause: nothing: left: nothing: afterthought

you

so you have no: desist quotas
you shall play misty for me and
I shall hunt you: down
   shall

take Pleistocene severities
and scudder you into: being
with the previous tools

what use a ship then? that
the quartan ague would that
the slum dengue would if:

not
the pitch toss hang us by
its typhus den. I:

shall have formed you by
recourse by: scrap loess
       by: pluvial hip
       by: scree

strained pee
fenugreekurial mustardy specks
in ear hem smeg. I:

shall have moulded all: various
all: husk circumspecks
all: correctnesses you:

shall try: decorum
gawdying leuchorea
bangles from bone grafts
anklets,
endearment waste,
haemoglobets,
scurf,
hedgerow DNA,
pre-cursory seepage. But I shall have:

already formed you
pinned displayed gorgeous
by your: odourless user name

you want the too

You punish me as a bandsaw would with your endless circuit dogteeth into me. You should simply tuck me under the bed. Your arse was a streprose smell gaged as a siphon-dribble, an aqueduct your moisture-escape trailing up the thigh. We divide our lives into many organisms but don't know which side the legs should be felled. There are seven gods to help us. These are: antigens, rheumoids, whorl algae, sequelae arbiters, pharyngismus repressors, the hinge fault corrector, a third eye. Nothing helps. I cry into mop-blankets. My cycle blood has made a mini-hawaii through two sheets to the mattress protector. Your filth was not of the graphite kind, soft, malleable, potentially decorous in its aftermath. But granite. Several hundred carvers squat and chisel hindu-icons from dawn until dusk from it. Ganesh cannot laugh you off for he is a ready-made and not organic as the other deities are. They line our coffin-slept place. Give me a tingible remnant so that I may pretend you still love me. You cannot hear the remnant-howls from there because you think you are found. There is cell death here and anything platform falls and all dust promises earth-wither. Your decision is rock. Igneous. Silicate. Basalt. It didn't matter how I did you, you still convinced me. You should have packed your holes when you left. They are deciduous and hoping and falling with the seasons' seconds. The minutes build to vast temples cut from a mountain. The pressure gauge resembles an upturned iceberg. There is no close-core the way we are scattered. I want your mucous membranes. I have only an old oilcloth and a severance talisman as an offering. Cast your cumwarning upon the air once more. We breathe a similitude. Coin to swine. Your pigsweet-meat creeps, crepuscular and haunting and I am squatting beneath iron bedsprings in a froth of mourning.

y/our affectuals

and cool for y/our stunted baneplace
to trace y/our history my bleedplane tool
to digskin burrow y/our psychefool seepcry spaces
to lameplay longnight seamspan incase anyplace just

cool for point fight muscle apathy for lathe celldeath prophesy
to graffitispray y/our closet doors tinsel blamename splay
to par potboil cherishing rubfever friction sway cool phew
to mewel against habit against remember-lay

cool for y/our depelt mistaken upon y/our runtboard pegs
to joyberry hurrystink along y/our live-lick saltdreg id
to smell derogatory slop crud smeg dread dregs
to lop y/our elevatorying loopskin rim dead

centre, then cool to crucify offspring withered capacity
to hobble, bootnail ghostshame and spewbottle illgain
to throttle neckthrob disdain too plaingotten pastpain
to enshrine y/our thus-veined y/our trustway y/our

cool y/our picklelove freezeframe y/our mute laid
dayjuiced shemale way: cool to sprottle you, spew-
cool to pray y/our witchsnatch unfought
because cool claim no fool

me way y/our you I can and wear my hot
in lieu of my cool for
you

AnnMarie Eldon, an identical twin, evolved from cryptophasic origins in once densely industrialised Birmingham, England. She was taught by her gypsy grandmother to say the alphabet backwards before the age of three. Juggling various *personae interiorae,* children and hormones and practicing counter-cultural reclusiveness, she achieves adult differentiation and spiritual equanimity within the mediocrity of a picturesque Oxfordshire market town, raising children, dogs and hope.